What, Me Incumbent?

by Jeff Danziger

A Third Collection of Political Cartoons from The Christian Science Monitor

Also by Jeff Danziger
Used Cartoons
Kinder, Gentler Cartoons

What, Me Incumbent?
Written and illustrated by Jeff Danziger

Library of Congress Catalog Card Number 92-074005
ISBN 0-87510-239-5

Forced to Get Serious

When I was in the army some years ago, the Gillette company brought out a self-heating shaving cream. You squirted the stuff into your hand, and as you waited in utter wonder, it got hot all by itself. I became devoted to this product in Vietnam, far from the comforts of hot water, but where I was still required, for some reason, to be clean shaven. Had I been blown apart by the North Vietnamese, part of me would have been as smooth as a baby's bottom.

Many barbers were put out of work by self-heating shaving cream. Other professions have been ruined by products which performed all by themselves. You hold in your hand what may be the cartoon equivalent of the straight razor. For we now live in an age of self-cartooning politicians.

Previously the politicians tried to lead the country seriously, and the cartoonists searched for humorous byplay, witty metaphor, and forced irony. Now, however, the politicians are hogging the entire act.

If anyone had suggested a cartoon of a cookie contest between candidates' wives, of a vice-president blaming a full-scale riot on a television sitcom, or of an American president annointing the prime minister of Japan in George Bush's unique manner, readers would have thought it ridiculous satire. Editors may reasonably have rejected such work as grotesque. But these things are accomplished by the subjects themselves.

Tom Wolfe noted that the problem with writing fiction in America these days was that fiction can't keep up with the truth. And the same is true with political cartoons. Every time you think you have a good, funny, fantastic idea, you find out the subject has already done it or said it that morning. And everyone is already laughing.

"What have you got for us this morning?" says your editor, looking at your hands for your daily offering.

"Um... err..." you say, having spotted your hilarious idea on the front page of that morning's paper, "... nothing."

I only mention this development because a large number of the cartoons in this collection are sort of somber. I have no choice. If all our politicians are going to be clowns, the cartoonists of the world will have to get serious.

Jeff Danziger

HOME TO ROOST
REAGANOMICS
GREED
DEALS
DEBT
THEFT
DANZIGER
The Christian Science Monitor
Los Angeles Times Syndicate

WHO LOST RUSSIA! WHO LOST RUSSIA!
WHO FOUND NIXON?
GOP
DANZIGER
The Christian Science Monitor
Los Angeles Times Syndicate

Leadership

OK... NOW..
DO NOTHING...
DEEPER
DEEPER
DEEPER
DEEPER
DANZIGER
The Christian Science Monitor
Los Angeles Times Syndicate

ALL HE HAS TO DO IS LOOK PRESIDENTIAL 'TIL NOVEMBER!
LOOK! HE'S DOING IT!
WE'RE SAVED!
DANZIGER
The Christian Science Monitor
Los Angeles Times Syndicate

BOY... I CAN'T TELL YOU HOW GOOD IT FEELS TO BE BACK AMONG FOREIGNERS!
UNITED STATES
DANZIGER
The Christian Science Monitor
Los Angeles Times Syndicate

THE VICE-PRESIDENT REVIEWS
BIO-TECH REGULATIONS
TOO COMPLICATED!
LOOK AT ALL THESE
LONG WORDS!
I'VE NEVER EVEN SEEN
SOME OF THESE WORDS!
QUAYLE
COMPETITIVENESS
COUNCIL
DANZIGER
The Christian Science Monitor
Los Angeles Times Syndicate

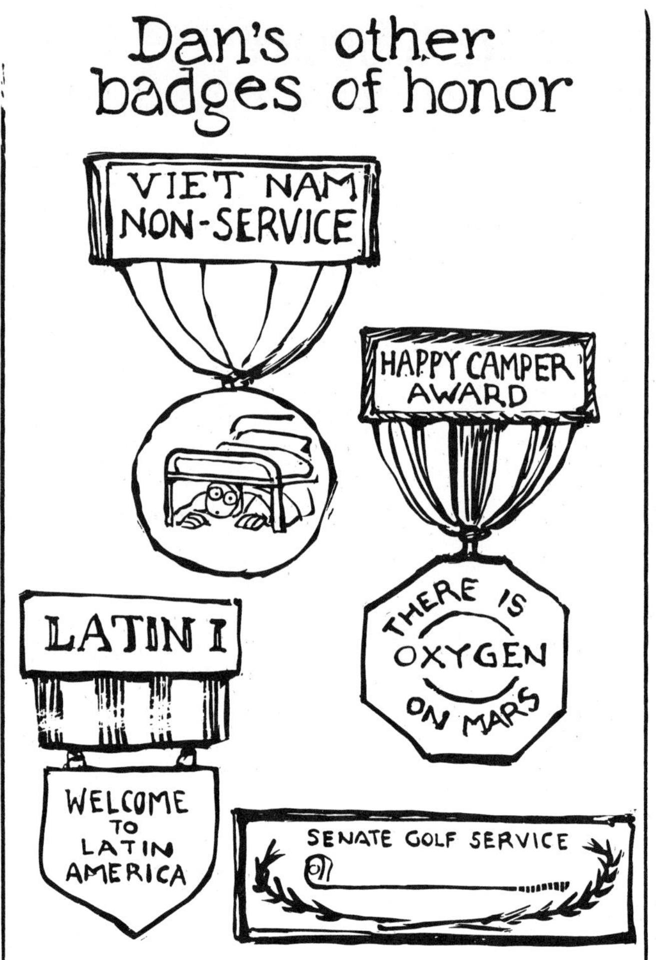

DANZIGER
The Christian Science Monitor
Los Angeles Times Syndicate

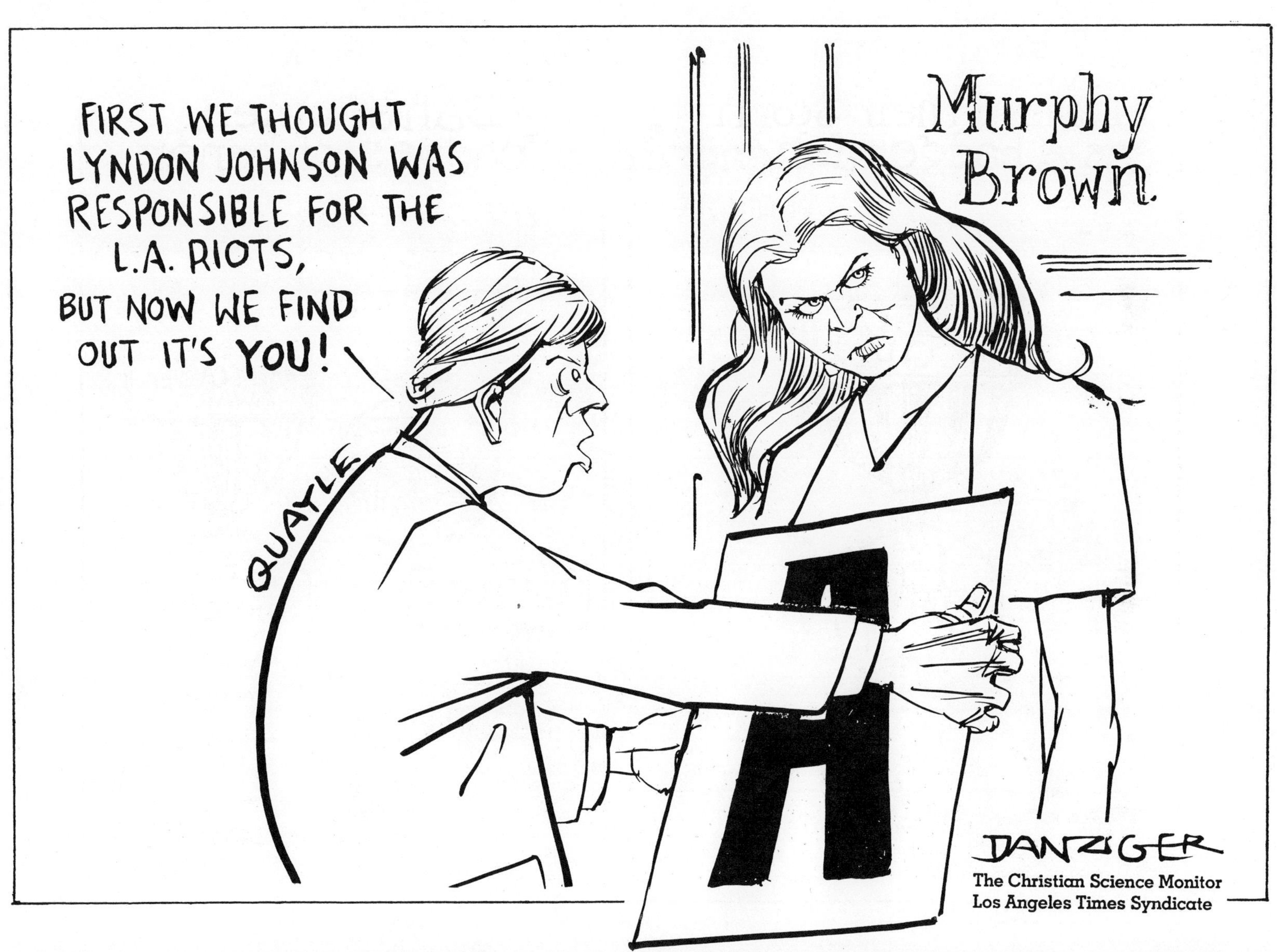
FIRST WE THOUGHT LYNDON JOHNSON WAS RESPONSIBLE FOR THE L.A. RIOTS, BUT NOW WE FIND OUT IT'S YOU!
Murphy Brown.
QUAYLE
A
DANZIGER
The Christian Science Monitor
Los Angeles Times Syndicate

The Christian Science Monitor
Los Angeles Times Syndicate

Power Lunch

THIS WILL BE GREAT, MR. PRESIDENT, JUST YOU AND ME AND JIM BAKER PUTTIN' OUR HEADS TOGETHER TO GET SOME IDEAS FOR THE CAMPAIGN ... JUST THE 3 OF US...
DAN
DANZIGER
The Christian Science Monitor
Los Angeles Times Syndicate

Los Angeles Times Syndicate

OF COURSE, THIS IS ALL
THE FAULT OF "McHALE'S NAVY."
HAITI
DANZIGER
The Christian Science Monitor
Los Angeles Times Syndicate

MR. BUSH CONSIDERS A FUTURE IN WHICH HE IS DEFEATED AND HAS TO WORK AS A CARPENTER ON LOW-INCOME HOUSING...

THE HORROR! THE HORROR!

DANZIGER

The Christian Science Monitor
Los Angeles Times Syndicate

ARIA

EXIT
MAKE UP?
IT'S ALL MADE UP...
I'VE WORKED MY HEART OUT!!
USED CARS
I'VE WORKED MY HEART OUT DOO-DAH DOO-DAH
COULD YOU MOVE? WE'RE STARTING NOW... MMMM... IS THAT EXTRA CRISPY?
DANZIGER
The Christian Science Monitor
Los Angeles Times Syndicate

BUSH QUAYLE FUND RAISER
DANZIGER
The Christian Science Monitor
Los Angeles Times Syndicate

5,000,000 CHILDREN HUNGRY IN U.S.
DON'T THINK of YOURSELF AS HUNGRY, THINK of YOURSELF AS LOW-FAT...
DANZIGER
The Christian Science Monitor
Los Angeles Times Syndicate

THE BUSH MEN, brothers and sons

OH, IF ONLY CONGRESS WEREN'T CONTROLLED BY THOSE DARN DEMOCRATS!
VETO
VETO
VETO
VETO
VETO
VETO
VETO
VETO
VETO
VETO
DANZIGER
The Christian Science Monitor
Los Angeles Times Syndicate

METAMORPHOSIS

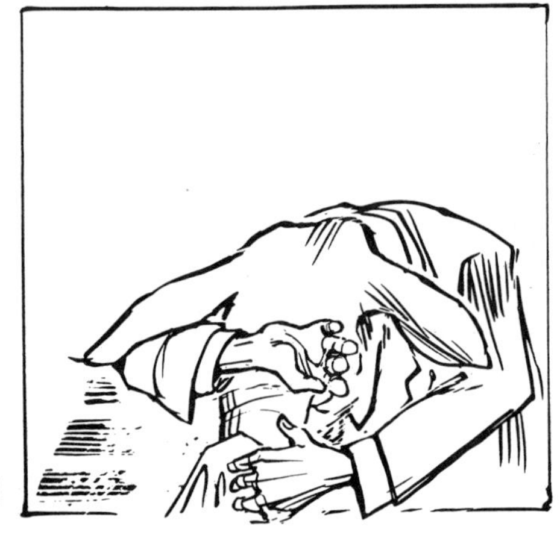

DANZIGER
The Christian Science Monitor
Los Angeles Times Syndicate

SURTAX ON RICH
MOTHER, FATHER SAYS THE DEMOCRATS ARE COMING FOR US. SHOULD I START PACKING?
DANZIGER
The Christian Science Monitor
Los Angeles Times Syndicate

BY THE WAY, SEEN MY GOVERNMENT LATELY?
THE TAX RAISE WAS A MISTAKE! OH... FORGIVE ME!
THE CHECK SCAM! A MISTAKE! NEVER HAPPEN AGAIN... ...REALLY...
CONGRESS
JANTUGER
The Christian Science Monitor
Los Angeles Times Syndicate

COLUMBIA TAKES OFF WITH SOME RATS AND JELLYFISH TO ANSWER THE SCIENTIFIC QUESTION...

... CAN CONGRESS SURVIVE IN SPACE?

The Christian Science Monitor

Smith-Corona, last US typewriter maker, moves to Mexico.
TH-CORONA CORPORATION
EMPLOYEE ENTRANCE
CLOSED
NOTICE
THIS PLANT WILL CLOSE AND MOVE TO MEXICO
HOWEVER!
YOU WILL BE PLEASED TO KNOW THAT A NEW
TACO BELL
WILL BE OPENING AT THIS LOCATION.
TRY OUR NAFTA GRANDE!
DANZIGER
The Christian Science Monitor
Los Angeles Times Syndicate

THE MOOD OF THE MIDDLE CLASS

1992

The Christian Science Monitor
Los Angeles Times Syndicate

Listening to America
Z
Z
Z
Z
HEY ROSS! GREAT TO TALK TO YOU! LONG TIME LISTENER! FIRST TIME CALLER! BOY, I BEEN WAITIN' ON THE LINE HERE FOR HOURS, BUT, HEY, IT'S GREAT TO GET TO TALK TO YOU, I MEAN LIKE, HERE I AM ON THE PHONE WITH A REAL BILLIONAIRE AN' SO... ... WHERE WAS I? OH, YEAH, WELL, ANYWAY, I GOT A COMMENT AN' A QUESTION, ACTUALLY TWO QUESTIONS, AND I'LL GIVE MY COMMENT AND THEN I'LL ASK MY QUESTION AND THEN I'LL ... WELL... I'LL... NOW, YOU KIDS STOP THAT! I'M ON THE PHONE..
DANZIGER
The Christian Science Monitor
Los Angeles Times Syndicate

Perot Quits

The Christian Science Monitor
Los Angeles Times Syndicate

YES... THE TIME TO BITE THE DEFICIT BULLET HAS COME... A TIME TO STREAMLINE OUR DEFENSES AND...
CLOSE FORT SNOOD?! THAT BASTION OF FREEDOM? THAT BULWARK OF LIBERTY? THAT SURE DEFENSE AGAINST COMMONISTS SNEAKIN' UP INTERSTATE 90 AND...
ATTACKING THE PX?
DANZIGER
The Christian Science Monitor

The Christian Science Monitor
Los Angeles Times Syndicate

Why I bounced checks

Some congressmen try to explain ...

DANZIGER

The Christian Science Monitor
Los Angeles Times Syndicate

CONGRESSMAN FLOOG IS TOLD WHAT REAL BANKS CHARGE FOR BOUNCED CHECKS

NEW ACCOUNTS

DANZIGER

The Christian Science Monitor
Los Angeles Times Syndicate

SCROOGE & GREENSPAN
DEC. 24
YOU'LL WANT ALL DAY OFF TOMORROW, I SUPPOSE...
WOE!
AWFUL NEWS
BAD NEWS
PRINCIPLES OF ECONOMICS
TODAY'S DIRECTION
DANZIGER
The Christian Science Monitor
Los Angeles Times Syndicate

MR. GREENSPAN TESTIFIES THAT THINGS WILL GET BETTER (PAUSE)

DANZIGER
The Christian Science Monitor
Los Angeles Times Syndicate

LATEST EXPERT TESTIMONY

THE SENATE FINANCE COMMITTEE HEARS FROM MADAM ZOG AND HER CRYSTAL BALL FOLLOWED BY BUZZY THE WONDER CAT, THING, AND AN UNIDENTIFIED GENTLEMAN FROM SANTA ANITA...

STICKER SHOCK
IMPORT
MADE IN JAPAN
4-DOOR SEDAN 14,000
DEALER PREP 600
SHIPPING 400
HIDDEN COSTS
GOVERNMENT PAYMENTS
TO US UNEMPLOYED 32,571
LOST REAL ESTATE
COMMUNITY TAXES 11,374
WELFARE PAYMENTS 15,304
FACTORIES CLOSED 12,712
SCHOOLS CLOSED 7,401
DECLINE IN US R&D 5,171
TRUE COST 99,533
DANZIGER
The Christian Science Monitor
Los Angeles Times Syndicate

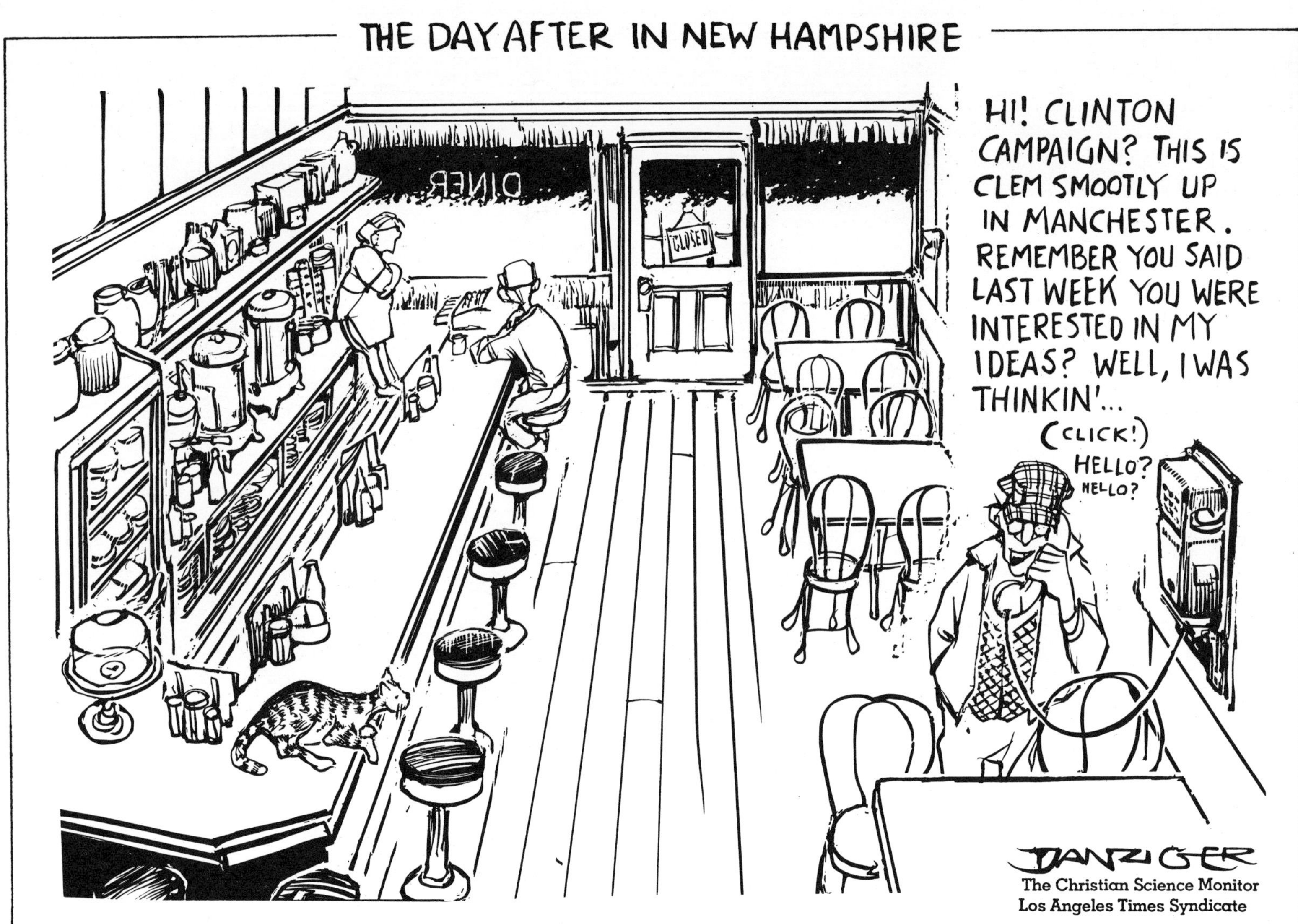
THE DAY AFTER IN NEW HAMPSHIRE
CLOSED
HI! CLINTON CAMPAIGN? THIS IS CLEM SMOOTLY UP IN MANCHESTER. REMEMBER YOU SAID LAST WEEK YOU WERE INTERESTED IN MY IDEAS? WELL, I WAS THINKIN'...
(CLICK!)
HELLO?
HELLO?
DANZIGER
The Christian Science Monitor
Los Angeles Times Syndicate

JERRY BROWN FOR CHANGE
NEW YORK! VOTE CLINTON VOTE CHANGE
AT LAST... AN IDEA WHOSE TIME HAS COME...
CHANGE, PLEASE?
FOR
AMERIC
6 DOWNTOWN
DANZIGER
The Christian Science Monitor

BUT ENOUGH ABOUT ME, BILL, LET'S HEAR WHAT YOU THINK OF MY PLAN FOR YOU...
CUOMO
DANZIGER
The Christian Science Monitor
Los Angeles Times Syndicate

THE CUOMO CAMPAIGN

The Christian Science Monitor
Los Angeles Times Syndicate

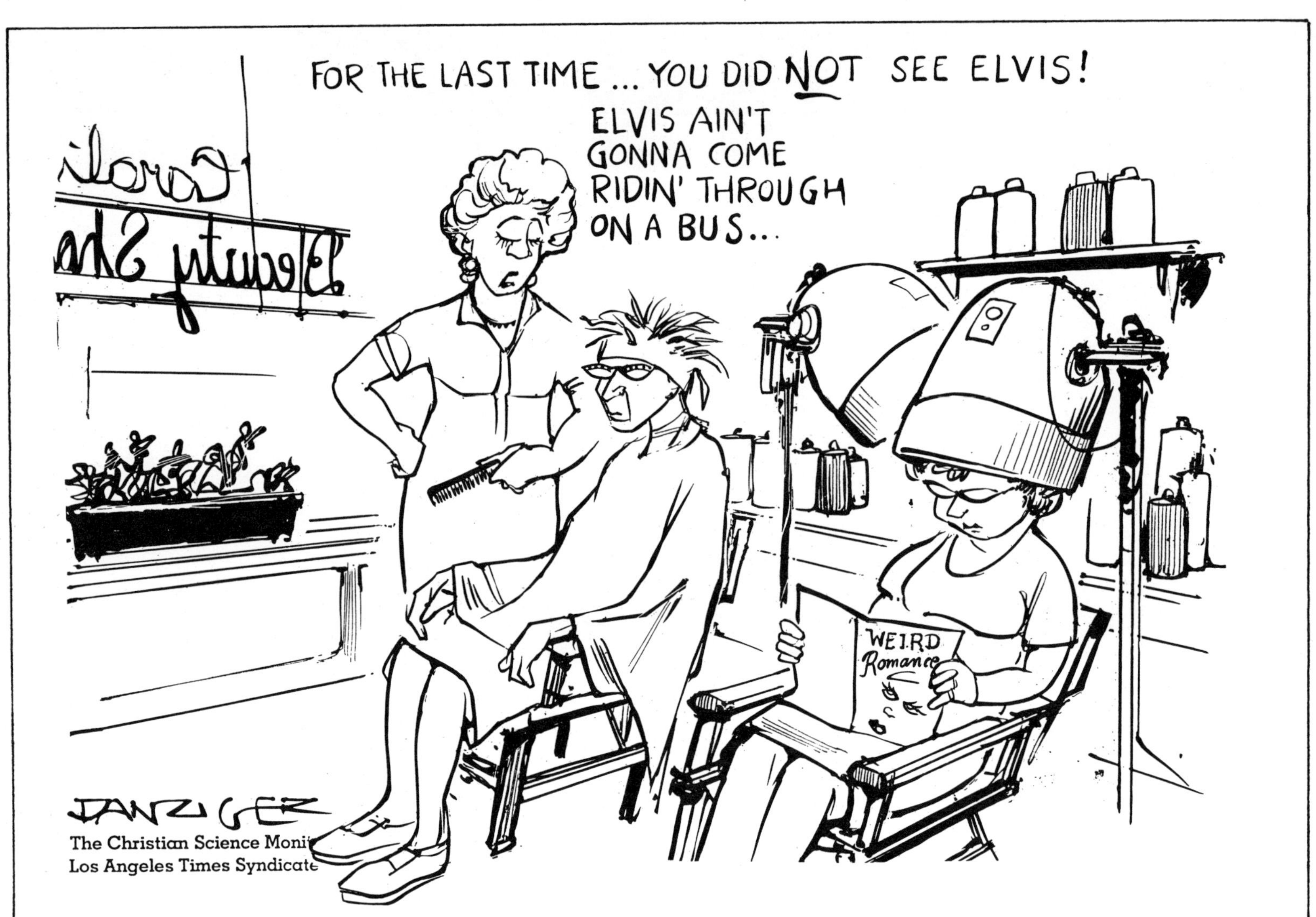
FOR THE LAST TIME ... YOU DID NOT SEE ELVIS!
ELVIS AIN'T GONNA COME RIDIN' THROUGH ON A BUS...
WEIRD Romance
DANZIGER
The Christian Science Monit
Los Angeles Times Syndicate

I DIDN'T KNOW IT WAS AN ALL-WHITE GOLF CLUB! I'LL NEVER PLAY GOLF AGAIN! I'LL PICK JESSE FOR VICE-PRESIDENT.. I'LL...
QUICK PLAN B...
HERE.
MAMMY
DANZIGER
The Christian Science Monitor
Los Angeles Times Syndicate

LET ME UNDERSTAND THIS, GOVERNOR CLINTON, YOU WANTED TO SERVE, BUT SOMEHOW THEY WOULDN'T LET YOU?
MY ARMY CAREER • VERSION 14
DANZIGER
The Christian Science Monitor
Los Angeles Times Syndicate

QUICK... WHERE ARE WE... AND WHAT DO THEY WANT TO HEAR ME SAY?
CLINTON FOR PRESIDENT
DANZIGER
The Christian Science Monitor
Los Angeles Times Syndicate

News
CLINTON'S SECRETS
OOOH!
OH, MY!
WHAT IS THIS?!
WHY DON'T YOU ASK THE OTHER CANDIDATES THESE QUESTIONS?
YES... ASK ME ABOUT MY STRATEGIC POLICY FOR INDUSTRIAL DEVELOPMENT...
...I'LL REVEAL THINGS THAT I NEVER TOLD MRS. TSONGAS...
DANZIGER
The Christian Science Monitor
Los Angeles Times Syndicate

The Tsongas Pronunciation Guide (a random tsample)

TSONG (noun)- mutsic with wordts. Example: The Tsar-tspangled Banner, "Oh, Tsay can you Tsee?"

TSELEVISION (noun) (also verb, adjective, adverb, preposition, conjunction and/or universal motivation.) Abbreviation: *Tseevee* as in, "I tsaw you on the *tseevee*. You should tsmile more."

BACKTSTABBER (noun) - What Bill Clinton said Jetsse Jacktson was. Then he said he was Tsorry. (Oh, tsure.)

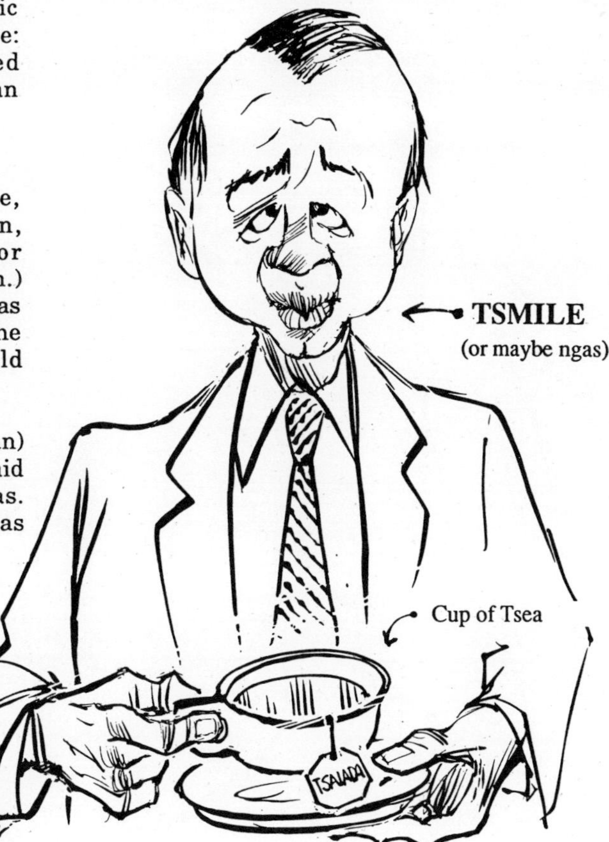

TSUPER TSUETSDAY - A big deal down in the Tsouth.

MATSSACHUTSETTS - Tsenator Tsongas's home tstate.

TSWIMMING - A tsport which proves you have a great deal of tstamina. As in, "I tsaw you tswimming on Tsunday, tso I will vote for you on Tsuetsday."

TSUSHI - what we will all be eating if we don't get rid of Butsh.

DANZIGER
The Christian Science Monitor
Los Angeles Times Tsyndicate

GREAT MOMENTS in AMERICAN LAW
HILLARY CLINTON'S FIRST BATCH OF COOKIES
HEY GALS! IMPRESS YOUR MAN!
SHARP COOKIE SCHOOL of LAW
"NUNC PRO TUNC"
DANZIGER
The Christian Science Monitor
Los Angeles Times Syndicate

OH, BARBARA DEAR, COULD YOU MAKE US SOME TEA AND COOKIES? WE'RE DISCUSSING TRADITIONAL AMERICAN VALUES!
YES, MY LOVE, HOW ABOUT SOME... (I CAN'T READ THIS.)
SNICKER-DOODLES
FOR THIS I MAJORED IN POLI-SCI?
SCRIPT
80 lbs. COOKIES
80 lbs. COOKIES
80 lb
TEA TEA
TEA TEA
DANZIGER
The Christian Science Monitor
Los Angeles Times Syndicate

HEY! THIS GUY BELONGS TO THE N.R.A. ...
...AND I BELONG TO THE WELL-REGULATED MILITIA...
NR
DANZIGER
The Christian Science Monitor

CHARLTON HESTON
NRA
BRADY BILL
DANZIGER
The Christian Science Monitor
os Angeles Times Syndicate

LIKE... EVERY YEAR THE TUITION GETS HIGHER ... AND EVERY YEAR THE WORK GETS HARDER...
SOMETHING U
...YEAH, LIKE WHAT'S THE MONEY FOR ?
DANZIGER
The Christian Science Monitor
Los Angeles Times Syndicate

KNOWLEDGE
REGISTRAR
THEY'RE THROWING US OUT INTO THE COLD, CRUEL WORLD!
THEY CALL IT GRADUATION.
DANZIGER
The Christian Science Monitor
Los Angeles Times Syndicate

NOW, MR. OBERST'S METHODS ARE SLIGHTLY OLD-FASHIONED, BUT HIS CLASSES HAVE THE HIGHEST MATH S.A.T.'S IN THE STATE...
Actung!
CHEATERS WILL BE SHOT
DANZIGER
The Christian Science Monitor
Los Angeles Times Syndicate

POLLS SHOW TSONGAS ONLY DOES WELL WITH EDUCATED VOTERS...
WHEW!
AND TO THINK HOW CLOSE WE CAME TO DOING SOMETHING ABOUT EDUCATION...
BUSH CAMPAIGN STRATEGY
☐ BREAD
☐ CIRCUSES
DANZIGER
The Christian Science Monitor
Los Angeles Times Syndicate

EFFICIENCY

JUSTICE

THE REHNQUIST COURT

The Christian Science Monitor
Los Angeles Times Syndicate

AS DIFFERENT AS BLACK AND BLACK
DANZIGER
The Christian Science Monitor
Los Angeles Times Syndicate

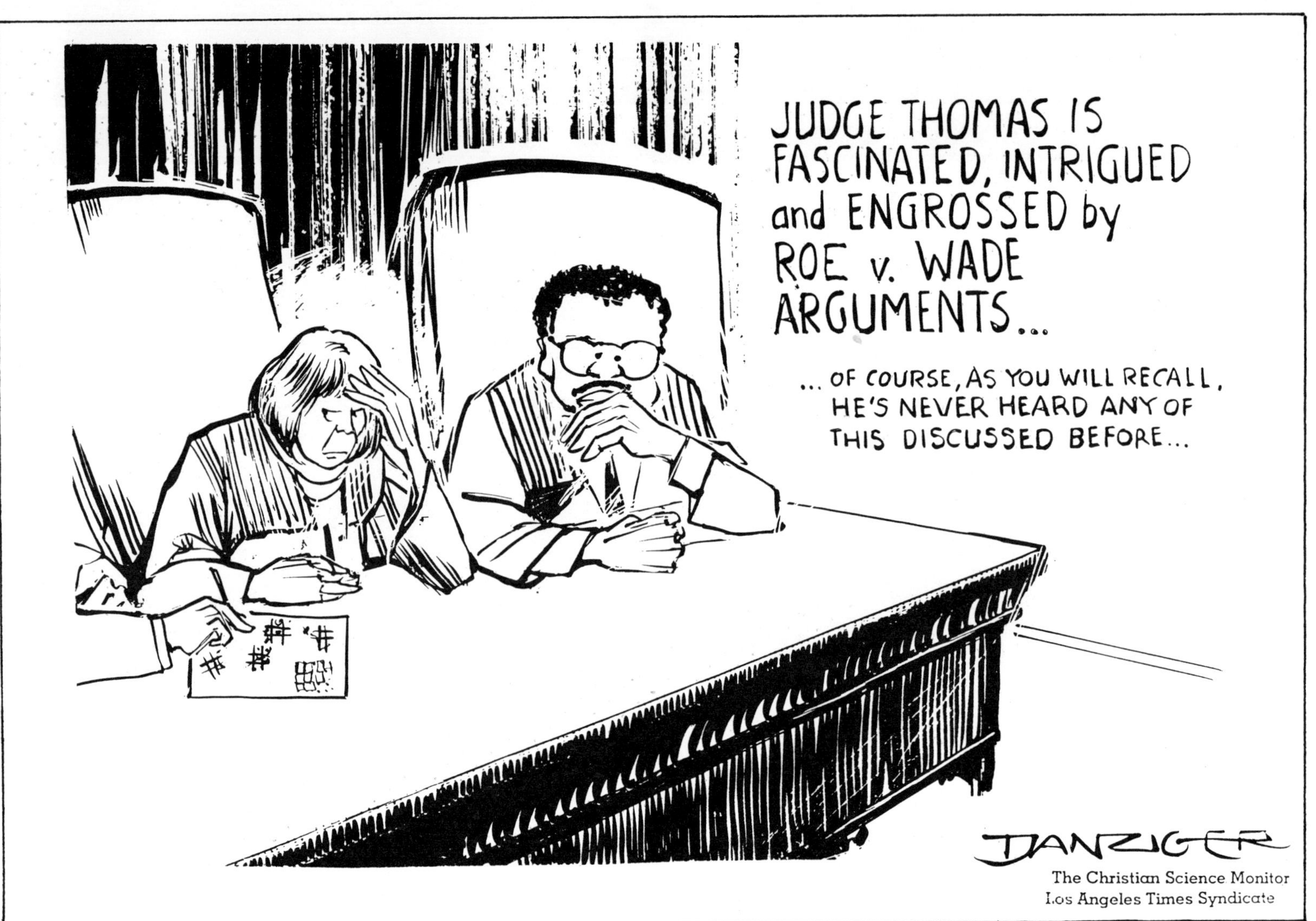
JUDGE THOMAS IS FASCINATED, INTRIGUED and ENGROSSED by ROE v. WADE ARGUMENTS...
... OF COURSE, AS YOU WILL RECALL, HE'S NEVER HEARD ANY OF THIS DISCUSSED BEFORE...
DANZIGER
The Christian Science Monitor
Los Angeles Times Syndicate

WE'VE MADE A PARTIAL CHANGE TO ROE v. WADE...
WITH PARTIAL SUPPORT
IN A PARTIAL MANNER
GIVING PARTIAL RIGHTS
TO A PART OF THE PEOPLE
WITH PARTIAL RESTRICTIONS
PARTIALLY EFFECTIVE
IN PART
FOR THE PARTIALLY PREGNANT...
DANZIGER
The Christian Science Monitor
Los Angeles Times Syndicate

SENATORS SPECTER, KENNEDY, HATCH, BIDEN LEAHY, SIMPSON, HEFLIN and THURMOND RE·CAP THE HEARINGS.

The Christian Science Monitor
Los Angeles Times Syndicate

AS AN ENDANGERED SPECIES YOURSELF, YOU MUST UNDERSTAND.
DANZIGER
The Christian Science Monitor
Los Angeles Times Syndicate

The Christian Science Monitor
Los Angeles Times Syndicate

ON DEATH ROW

NO LUCK ON YOUR APPEAL... ELECTION YEAR Y'KNOW...
DANZIGER
The Christian Science Monitor
Los Angeles Times Syndicate

NEWSPAPERS • MAGAZINES
Caress
GIRL WHIRL
Together
PARTY TIME!
Whoopie MAGAZINE
NIGHTLIFE
GLAMOUR
LOVE
PIZZAZZ
SMOOCH MAGAZINE
APPEAL
WING-DING
BEAUTY
BODY!
Romance MAGAZINE
ME MAGAZINE
"...LATEST THING..."
ABSTINENCE MAGAZINE
DANZIGER
The Christian Science Monitor
Los Angeles Times Syndicate

MANAGEMENT EXPLAINS WHY WE MUST MAKE RIGHT-HAND DRIVE CARS

DANZIGER
The Christian Science Monitor
Los Angeles Times Syndicate

MEMBERS. NEW YORK STOCK EXCHANGE
THE END OF THE WORLD?
WELL, SURE...
...BUT WE FEEL THE
MARKET HAS
ALREADY DISCOUNTED
THAT...
DANZIGER
The Christian Science Monitor
Los Angeles Times Syndicate

Dee Dee's NEW JOB...

The Christian Science Monitor
Los Angeles Times Syndicate

ECONOMISTS SAY MANUFACTURING SECTOR MAY SPARK THE RECOVERY
WHAT?
IT'S FLOOGLE! HE MADE SOMETHING!
IT'S A THING! A REAL THING!
MADE IN USA!
MY! MY!
WE'RE SAVED! CALL WASHINGTON!
LOOK AT IT!
WHAT IS IT?
WHO CARES? AT LEAST IT'S NOT A HAMBURGER...
DANZIGER
The Christian Science Monitor
Los Angeles Times Syndicate

...JUST LIKE WALL STREET IN THE 80'S
DANZIGER
The Christian Science Monitor
Los Angeles Times Syndicate

WHAT I DON'T UNDERSTAND IS WHY THESE PEOPLE DESTROY THEIR OWN HOMES...
WE'D NEVER DO THAT...
DANZIGER
The Christian Science Monitor
Los Angeles Times Syndicate

I THINK I'M GROWING UP...
I CAN LOOK AT HOMELESS PEOPLE
AND FEEL NOTHING...
DANZIGER
The Christian Science Monitor
Los Angeles Times Syndicate

HEALTH CARE in AMERICA
CHECK BOOK
DANZIGER
The Christian Science Monitor
Los Angeles Times Syndicate

Mr. GINGRICH, HAPPY AT LAST

NOW, THIS IS ART!
NO SMOKING
SEN. HELMS
HEY 3rd WORLD
Made in USA
LIGHT 'EM UP!
PAID FOR BY US TAXPAYERS
DANZIGER
The Christian Science Monitor
Los Angeles Times Syndicate

The Christian Science Monitor
Los Angeles Times Syndicate

AT THE PENTAGON
PROGRAM CUTBACKS, BASE CLOSINGS, THIS IS WHAT WE GET FOR WINNING THE COLD WAR...
YEAH, WHOSE DUMB IDEA WAS THAT?
POOR PLANNING, VERY POOR PLANNING...
DANZIGER
The Christian Science Monitor
Los Angeles Times Syndicate

I LIKE TO READ THIS PART, OVER AND OVER AND OVER...
WAR
THE BALKANS
HISTORY
DANZIGER
The Christian Science Monitor
Los Angeles Times Syndicate

MADAM... I ASSURE YOU WE'RE DOING EVERYTHING WE CAN TO END YOUR SUFFERING.
ARMS MAKERS
U.S., BRITISH, GERMAN, ITALIAN ISRAELI, CHINESE ETC.
SOMALIA
DANZIGER
The Christian Science Monitor
Los Angeles Times Syndicate

AMERICAN CORPORATE EXECUTIVES GO SIGHTSEEING IN TOKYO...

WHEW... FOR A MOMENT I THOUGHT IT WAS "SAVE THE WHALES."

NOW LEE, YOU JUST SMILE AND THINK OF AIR BAGS...
IACOCCA
NEXT GUY WHO CALLS ME "YUM-YUM" GETS THE PARASOL, HARD...
3 LITTLE MAIDS FROM
Ford
GM
DANZIGER
The Christian Science Monitor
Los Angeles Times Syndicate

YOU BORROWED ON INFLATED STOCKS TO BUY INFLATED REAL ESTATE ?
BOY! YOU JAPANESE GOTTA STOP COPYIN' US...
JAPANESE MARKETS IN FREE FALL
Coke
YES! WE TAKE FOOD STAMPS
DANZIGER
The Christian Science Monitor
Los Angeles Times Syndicate

JIM BAKER LOOKS THE JAPANESE RIGHT IN THE EYE!

BUY AMERICAN PLEASE? PRETTY PLEASE?!

The Christian Science Monitor
Los Angeles Times Syndicate

The Christian Science Monitor
Los Angeles Times Syndicate

... NATURALLY WE MUST CONTINUE TO STRIVE FOR WAYS TO MAKE ADDITIONAL EFFORTS SO AS TO EFFECT METHODS FOR A BETTER UNDERSTANDING OF ROUTES TOWARD APPROACHES TO SOLUTIONS WHICH WILL BRING ABOUT A DIALOGUE FROM WHICH...
DON'T STOP... HE'S STILL BREATHING.
TORA TORA TORA
TRADE TALKS
US PRODUCTS
DANZIGER
The Christian Science Monitor
Los Angeles Times Syndicate

DANZIGER
The Christian Science Monitor
Los Angeles Times Syndicate
CHINESE EXPORTS

OF COURSE, AS WE CHINESE MOVE TOWARD CAPITALISM, WE RETAIN SOME OF THE TRADITIONS OF COMMUNISM...
DANZIGER
The Christian Science Monitor
Los Angeles Times Syndicate

Mr. BAKER
Thank you FOR FINDING ME
YITZHAK... BELIEVE ME, IF YOU GET LOST IN THE DESERT WE'LL LOOK FOR YOU, TOO...
JANZIGER
The Christian Science Monitor
Los Angeles Times Syndicate

ISRAEL
YOU LIVE YOUR LIFE. YOU BUILD UP A PLACE. YOU MIND YOUR OWN BUSINESS
SHAMIR
SYRIA
JOR
LEBAN
YOU HATE THE NEIGHBORS. THEY HATE YOU. IT'S A LIVING.
JOR
SYRI
LEBAN
THEN ALONG COMES MISTER FRIENDLY.
HI... JIM BAKER. PEACE IS MY PROFESSION.
COME... LET US BREAK BREAD. LET US REASON TOGETHER. LET US BE BROTHERS. LET
OY...
DANZIGER
The Christian Science Monitor
Los Angeles Times Syndicate

NO ROCKS
PLEASE,
WE
VOTED
LABOR
DANZIGER
The Christian Science Monitor
Los Angeles Times Syndicate

The Christian Science Monitor
Los Angeles Times Syndicate

IRAQ
MILITARY
MADE IN
USA
DANZIGER
The Christian Science Monitor
Los Angeles Times Syndicate

COME IN! COME IN!
INSPECT! INSPECT!
ALL WE NEEDED WAS A LITTLE TIME TO CLEAN THE PLACE.. ...IRAQI HOSPITALITY YOU KNOW...
I'LL GO MAKE TEA...
SADDAM
ELECTROLUX
DANZIGER
The Christian Science Monitor
Los Angeles Times Syndicate

BREAD
WE DON'T HAVE TO WORRY ABOUT THE RUSSIANS... THEY LOVE COLD WEATHER.
THE WEST
DANZIGER
The Christian Science Monitor
Los Angeles Times Syndicate

DANZIGER
The Christian Science Monitor
Los Angeles Times Syndicate

FINALLY UNEMPLOYED, MIKHAIL GORBACHEV MOVES TO CAVENDISH, VERMONT WHERE HE OPENS A BP STATION WITH ALEKSANDR SOLZHENITSYN...
S&G
QUICK STOP
Coca Cola
VIDEO RENTALS
SANDWICHES
GROCERIES
COFFEE
TOYOTA
ZEREX
DANZIGER
The Christian Science Monitor
Los Angeles Times Syndicate

DESPERATE FOR FUN, RUSSIANS BUILD LENIN SNOWMEN
YOU GOT CARROT?
FOR LUNCH.
FOR NOSE?
DANZIGER
The Christian Science Monitor
Los Angeles Times Syndicate

JUST WHEN YOU GET IN THE TUB, THE PHONE RINGS...
BLACK SEA FLEET
YELTSIN
МАТЬ
IT'S NATO. WHO'S IN CHARGE?
KRAVCHUK
DANZIGER
The Christian Science Monitor
Los Angeles Times Syndicate

LATEST NEWS: MIR SPACE STATION DECLARES INDEPENDENCE FROM SOVIET UNION
МИР
INDEPENDENT REPUBLIC OF OUTER ORBITIA
DANZIGER
The Christian Science Monitor
Los Angeles Times Syndicate

Boris returns...
WHAT DID YOU BRING ME?
WHAT DID YOU BRING ME?
WHAT DID YOU BRING ME?
WHAT DID YOU BRING ME?
WHAT DID YOU BRING ME?
WHAT DID YOU BRING ME?
WHAT DID YOU BRING ME?
BORIS WENT TO USA AND ALL I GOT WAS THIS STOOPID T-SHIRT
DANZIGER
The Christian Science Monitor
Los Angeles Times Syndicate

YELTSIN SAYS THERE MAY BE VIETNAM ERA US P.O.W.'S IN SOVIET PRISONS

WELCOM
CZECHOS
HAVEL
BITTE?
DANZIGER
The Christian Science Monitor
Los Angeles Times Syndicate

SERBS OUT
AT LAST... I MISS COMMUNISM...
DANZIGER
The Christian Science Monitor
Los Angeles Times Syndicate

THE GREAT HEART of AMERICA GOES OUT TO THE POOR RUSSIANS WHO HAVE TO GET THROUGH THE WINTER WITHOUT SODA, FROZEN PIZZA, CHIPS or VIDEOS...
BY GEORGE, WE GOTTA HELP THOSE PEOPLE!
BEAN DIP
GIDGET
BULLITT
The OMEN
DANZIGER
The Christian Science Monitor
Los Angeles Times Syndicate

SO, WHAT'S ON FOR TOMORROW? YOUR GUY INSULTS OUR GUY OR OUR GUY INSULTS YOUR GUY?
TOGETHER WE CAN DO ANYTHING
DANZIGER
The Christian Science Monitor
Los Angeles Times Syndicate

HISTORIC MARKER · SARAJEVO

Ms. TUTWILER EXPLAINS US-BOSNIA POLICY
...TUT-TUT...
US
POLICY
DANZIGER
The Christian Science Monitor
Los Angeles Times Syndicate

GERMAN DIPLOMACY in YUGOSLAVIA
YOO HOO! VEE RECOGNIZE CROATS!
UND VEE RECOGNIZE SERBS!
COME ON OUT!
UND DON'T SCRATCH THE CAR, YOU HOODLUMS...
DANZIGER
The Christian Science Monitor
Los Angeles Times Syndicate

COMMUNISM WAS VERY BAD.
IF IT WEREN'T FOR COMMUNISM,
WE COULD HAVE BEEN DOING THIS
YEARS AGO...
DANZIGER
The Christian Science Monitor
Los Angeles Times Syndicate

Baseball Salaries
Explained...
$274.35
DANZIGER
The Christian Science Monitor
Los Angeles Times Syndicate

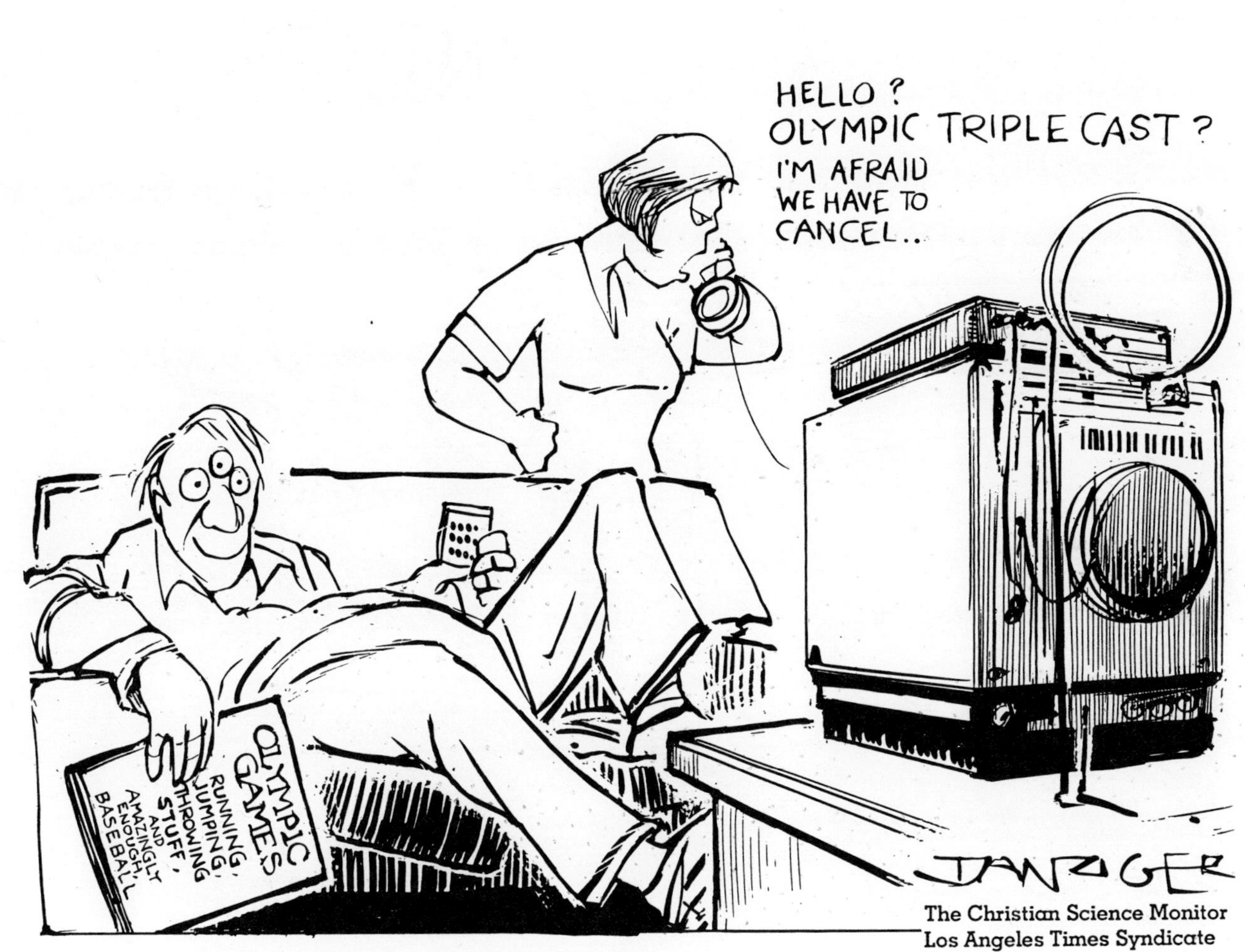
HELLO ?
OLYMPIC TRIPLE CAST ?
I'M AFRAID
WE HAVE TO
CANCEL..
OLYMPIC GAMES
RUNNING,
JUMPING,
THROWING
STUFF,
AND
AMAZINGLY
ENOUGH,
BASEBALL
DANZIGER
The Christian Science Monitor
Los Angeles Times Syndicate

Your new New York cabbie

THE EPA SAYS LAWNMOWERS ARE MAJOR POLLUTERS

THE OTHER DAY
UPON THE STAIR,
I MET A MAN
WHO WASN'T THERE.
HE WASN'T THERE
AGAIN TODAY.
I WISH, I WISH
HE'D GO AWAY.
CLINTON DRAFT RECORD
DANZIGER
The Christian Science Monitor
Los Angeles Times Syndicate

THE DEBATE SO FAR ...
CLINTON
CHA NEW
IDEAS · POLICIES
PROGRAMS
THE FUTURE
ROTC!
ROTC!
ROTC!
ROTC!
ROTC!
ROTC!
DANZIGER
The Christian Science Monitor
Los Angeles Times Syndicate

UN VOTES TO EJECT YUGOSLAVIA

ETHNIC FREEZING

WELCOME BACK TO "ROSS PEROT LIVE" WITH MY GUEST LARRY KING..
DANZIGER
The Christian Science Monitor
Los Angeles Times Syndicate

ROSS PEROT
FOR PRESIDENT
OR SOMETHING
IT'S ME! THE BOSS IS BACK!
HEY, LOOK! IT'S WHATSHISFACE...
PAID VOLUNTEER
YOU GOT YOUR CHECK-BOOK WITH YOU, BOSS?
PEROT
HOT DOGS
MUST
BREAD
DANZIGER
The Christian Science Monitor
Los Angeles Times Syndicate

The Christian Science Monitor
Los Angeles Times Syndicate

I DO BELIEVE IN HARRY TRUMAN – I DO BELIEVE IN HARRY TRUMAN – I DO
SPURT of AMERICA
DANZIGER
The Christian Science Monitor
Los Angeles Times Syndicate

US
ECONOMY
OH! SO YOU DON'T BELIEVE I CAME DOWN THE CHIMNEY?
SMART ALEC! YOU PROBABLY DON'T BELIEVE IN TAX CREDITS, EITHER...
DANZIGER
The Christian Science Monitor
Los Angeles Times Syndicate

MR. KISSINGER TESTIFIES ON POW'S LEFT BEHIND in VIETNAM
IS THIS THE TRUTH, HENRY?
OR THE USUAL?
DANZIGER
The Christian Science Monitor
Los Angeles Times Syndicate

The Christian Science Monitor
Los Angeles Times Syndicate

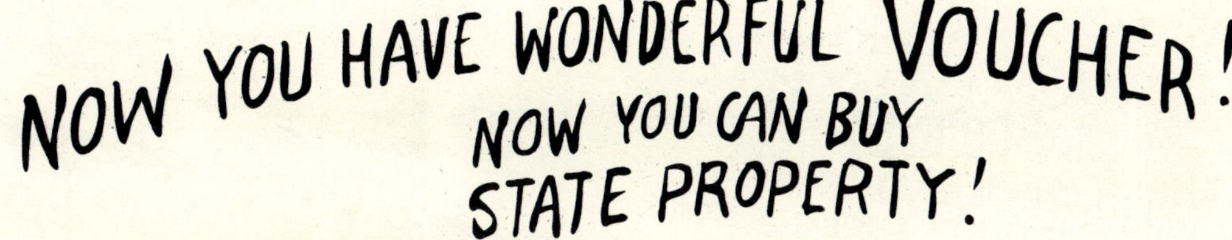

The Christian Science Monitor
Los Angeles Times Syndicate

AND NOW MR. BUSH WILL PLAY A STIRRING TUNE OF FREEDOM, JUSTICE AND LIBERTY WHICH WILL EMBOLDEN OUR CHINESE FRIENDS IN THEIR GLORIOUS QUEST FOR DEMOCRACY.
CHOPSTICKS
STEINWAY
DANZIGER
The Christian Science Monitor
Los Angeles Times Syndicate

WELL, GEORGE, OUR ACCOUNTANT SAYS WE'VE GOT BACK ALL THE MONEY WE LOST TO ROOSEVELT...
SO MAYBE IT'S NOT CRUCIAL THAT YOU WIN...
$
DANZIGER
The Christian Science Monitor
Los Angeles Times Syndicate

UH... YES... WE'VE SEEN THE POLLS.
SEAL OF THE PRESIDENT OF THE UNITED STATES
DANZIGER
The Christian Science Monitor
Los Angeles Times Syndicate